SOUL
searching for one

Dear friend,

You are holding more than just a journal.

You are holding pages that are meant to be filled with life.

There is no right or wrong way to use this journal.

Write down your own poems.

Scribble down the lyrics to your favorite tunes.

Draw.

Sketch.

Feel.

Turn this journal into an illustrated book.

Use the printed art as a visual prompt.

Or don't.

Write horizontally.

Vertically.

Fill the blank page.

Make the printed art a part of your creation.

Let your creativity take the lead.

it's time to create beautiful things
with rough edges and smooth undertones
perfectly imperfect
they shine or flow or sink
right into one's heart
they make you feel
pour them all over
the page
it's your time to start

Katya Ederer

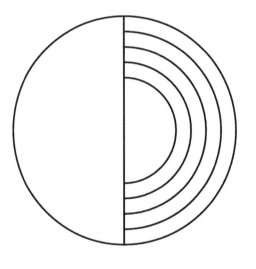

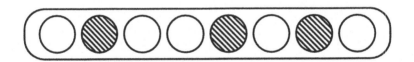

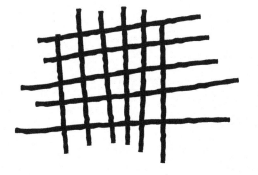

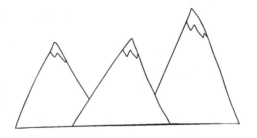

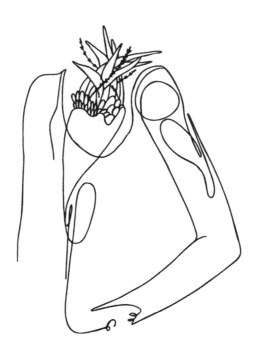

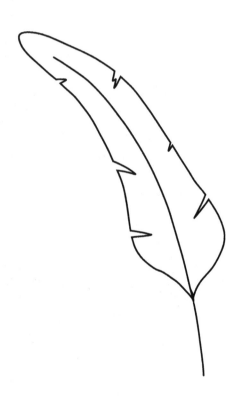

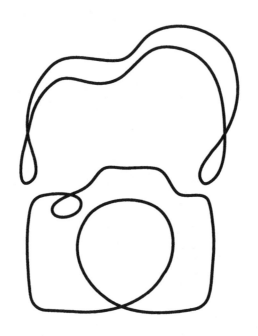

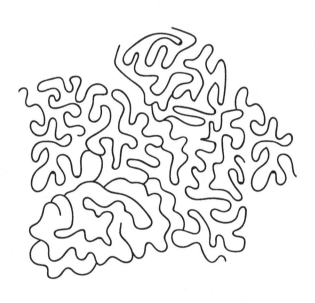

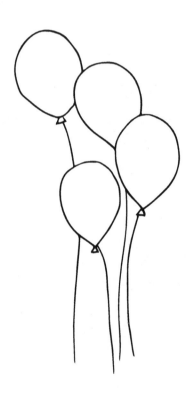

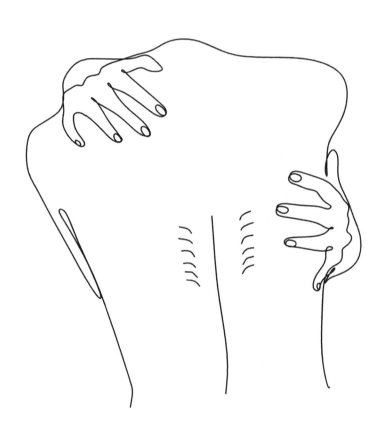

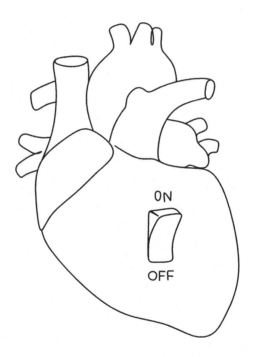

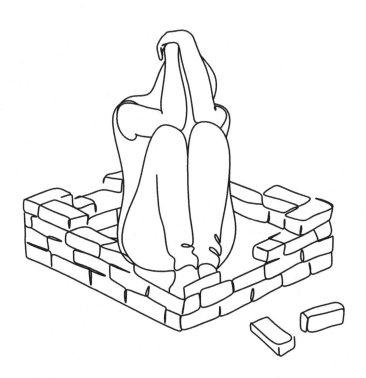

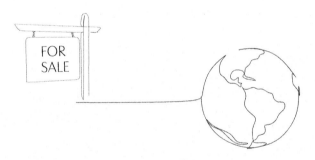

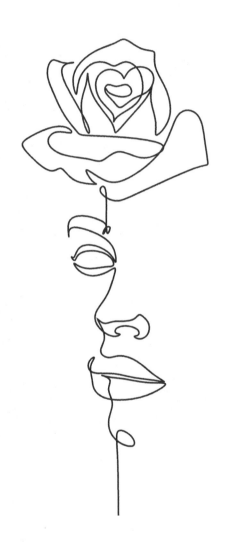

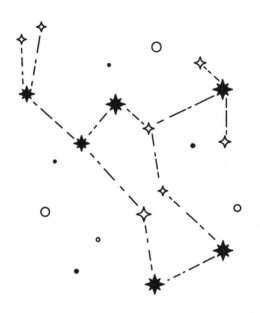

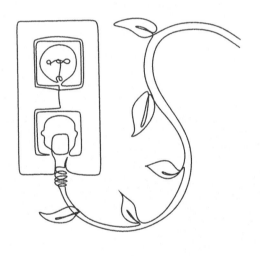

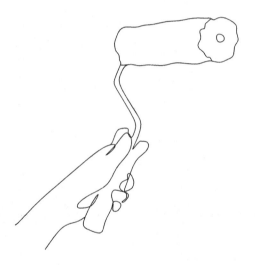

Made in the USA
Las Vegas, NV
20 August 2022

53673465R00059